cotton candy
on a rainy
day

by Nikki Giovanni

poems by
nikki giovanni

cotton candy on a rainy day

WILLIAM MORROW AND COMPANY, INC.

NEW YORK   1978

Library of Congress Cataloging in Publication Data

Giovanni, Nikki.
    Cotton candy on a rainy day.

    I. Title.
PS3557.I55C6   811'.5'4   78-16897
ISBN 0-688-03365-2

BOOK DESIGN   CARL WEISS

Printed in the United States of America

First Edition

1   2   3   4   5   6   7   8   9   10

FOR

GUS

CONTENTS

INTRODUCTION

A Woman of the Seventies

I HAVE A PICTURE IN MY MIND FROM THE SIXTIES OF NIKKI Giovanni. I had only recently met her and I, along with others, was sitting in the back of a car; Nikki and the driver were up front. One of the riders in the back wanted Nikki to read some poetry of hers. "I can't," said Nikki. "I get motion sickness." It was quite some time before I understood that of all Nikki's faults, and they are there, indirectness is not among them. We laughed that day thinking Nikki had put someone down. The fact was and is—she gets motion sickness. A lot of what Nikki says and does has to be taken at face value. Words, indeed, are that precious to her. She uses them both correctly and accurately.

Ida Lewis, one of Nikki's closest friends, likes to tell the story of Nikki's "bravery." Ida, who is publisher of *Encore American & Worldwide News* magazine, and Nikki, along with a secretary from the magazine, decided they wanted to have an ice-cream soda one winter's evening in the early seventies. Ida had broken her ankle in a fall on ice and was on crutches.

11

Deciding to give themselves a royal treat the three of them went to an ultrachic ice-cream parlor on Manhattan's East Side. No sooner had their order arrived than Ida overheard the owner say to his cashier: "Clear the place; we have a bomb in here." Ida, as she tells the story, calmly said to Nikki: "There's a bomb in here." And before "here" could leave Ida's lips Nikki had picked up her coat, her ever-present briefcase, Ida's coat and briefcase and was on the sidewalk. Ida, of course, gives a pitiful picture of herself struggling with crutches to get out of the place. It really takes Tommy, Nikki's son, to describe Ida's hobbling during that period. Even now the story brings tears of laughter to Ida's eyes. When Ida tells that story Nikki gets that "here she goes again" expression that is a combination both of anxiety that she will be misunderstood and amusement at a very funny tale. "But Ida," Nikki invariably points out, "I thought you were right behind me." A lot of people in Nikki's life, I think, have heard the same explanation.

But it takes the playwright Clay Goss, our mutual friend, to tell the Nikki stories. He can give any speech of hers with all the gestures and nuances intact. Clay is a big man, tall, ex-football player, deep bass voice. When he stands to do his imitation of "Space Nikki," concluding with all the universe reciting "Ego Tripping," tears are rolling down our eyes. He really ought to put that on stage. *Cotton Candy on a Rainy Day* brings a different Nikki to us.

Where does a poem begin? There are several esoteric theories but all are vulnerable to the times the poet has lived through and is living in. For young Blacks, whose sensibilities were formed in the crucible of the sixties, a poem did not begin in the mind or even the heart; it was stunned into life by the eye. We saw so much in such a short space of time, from burning hearts to burning cities. The eye was the center of that storm. The eye was the means to sort out the daily dramas of that period, which flipped before us in cinematographic frames. The poetry of that period recorded what we saw, more than

what we felt. But the sixties mostly made us look within ourselves and we recognized the noblest of our spirit, the courage
inherent in rebellion, the reawakening of pride buried deep
in our unconscious memories. But the other face was there
too: the face of forgotten hatreds and fears, the face which
dropped its eyes in the light of the heroic moment, the face
which tried to fill emptiness with politics rather than comfort.
Pride and shame, courage and compromise, hate and love all
came together in one volatile and fragile Black soul. Some
survived the explosion and grew. Others chose to snap off
the light in front of the mirror.

Nikki Giovanni is a witness. Her intelligent eye has caught
the experience of a generation and dutifully recorded it. She
has seen enough heroes, broken spirits, ironies, heartless minds
and mindless hearts to fill several lifetimes.

To Nikki, poems are not precious jewels to be constantly
compared to more flawless gems. They are not something to
be mulled over and polished until they show no resemblance
to the earth from which they came. Rather they are thought
of as souvenirs extracted from the site of some precious moment.
Their value is in the experience that it recalls:

> i shall save my poems
> for the winter of my dreams

If the reception to her other books is any indication this
one will be met with great anticipation from critics, book re-
viewers, rivals and friends. Like the others, the opinions about
Cotton Candy will be controversial, whether in print or private
conversation. Is it as good as the last book? Is Nikki Giovanni
still the same Nikki we knew before? Is it good poetry? Is it
good Black poetry? I suspect that Nikki will have only a mild
interest in the answers. She cares about how her work is re-
ceived, as any mother cares about the public reaction to her
child, though the more personal criticism will be summarily
dismissed. Unfortunately, if the past is any indicator, few
of those comments will take into account Nikki's attitude
toward her work.

Craft is important to her. But in her view one good line in a poem makes it valuable, and, conversely, an imperfect line does not make it valueless. I have heard Nikki say that if one day our civilization were reduced to rubble and if her poems were found among the ruins, she hopes that they would reveal something of our lives here. Not just the grand philosophical concepts, but the smaller things too, which may be less noble but are as important truths as any. One may, for example, learn just as much about the French by their eating habits as by reading their great philosophers. Our idiosyncracies, our involuntary reflexes, the imperfect stroke is often the signature of a work because it makes it unique and personal—like a fingerprint:

> but i sit writing
> a poem
> about my habits
> which while it's not
> a great poem
> is mine

It is not important to her that her poems live in greatness, but that they live. That they have the force to pull someone in who may say, "Yes. I have felt that way. No. I am not alone." That is their great test. The heart, not the form, is the final arbiter.

It is an arrogant philosophy in its own way. But it has also made her one of the most important contemporary poets and one of the few who can still fill an auditorium. Her poetry has led many of her readers to cross many emotional bridges from Black militancy to having the wherewithal to say something is wrong when politics, not people, become the priority. She is an honest poet and believes in confronting the big issues as well as the secret insecurities. It's just like Nikki to turn an anxious corner of her life—reaching thirty—by celebrating her birthday with a concert at Lincoln Center.

In *Cotton Candy on a Rainy Day* the reader will see another side of the Nikki Giovanni we saw in her previous books. The militant poems are long gone, which is not to say that she no

14

longer stands by them but that they are the truth of another
time. The sassy, hand-on-the-hip love poems are also scarce
though there is the familiar sense of mischief-making in one:

> if you've got the key
> then i've got the door
> let's do what we did
> when we did it before

Cotton Candy is the most introspective book to date, and the
most plaintive. It speaks of loneliness, personal emptiness
and love which is not unrequited but, even worse, misunderstood and misbegotten. The mood is not despair or self-pity.
It is more the pensive that comes from realizing that another
cycle of one's life has been completed:

> ... Now i don't fit
> beneath the rose bushes
> anymore

But in Nikki's words life is "not a problem but a process" and

> anyway they're gone

Inevitably, the shining innocence that comes from feeling the
ideal is possible is also gone, and one must learn to live with less:

> she had lived both long and completely enough
> not to be chained to the truth ...
> she had no objections to the lies
> ... like i need you

And in another poem:

> she decided to become
> a woman
> and though he still refused
> to be a man
> she decided it was all
> right

The loneliness carries no blame, no bitterness, just the reali-
zation of a void:

> i could say i am black female
> and bright
> in a white mediocre world
> but that hardly explains why
> i sit on the beaches of st croix
> feeling so abandoned

Cotton Candy is the private moments: of coming to terms with oneself—of living with oneself. Taken in the context of Nikki's work it completes the circle: of dealing with society, others and finally oneself.

Does this book of poetry reveal much about Nikki? As much as the other things she has chosen to surround her: the Black paintings and nineteenth-century prints; the photos of her son; the books, everything from *I, Claudius* to the latest from James McPherson, from the *Kennedy Reader* to *Country Inns & Back Roads*—a guide to restaurants off the beaten path. They all reflect a side of her. They all document her ever-widening world.

"I want you to travel," Nikki tells her audiences from New Brunswick, New Jersey, to Normal, Alabama, to Chico, California. "When you graduate and get that plastic money buy an experience instead of a thing." Nikki, then looking every bit the elf she can be, says, "Anyway," laughing now, "if you buy something and you go broke they can take it from you. Buy yourself a trip or a hundred-dollar meal and it's yours forever." The audience laughs with her. They know, these college youngsters, how much they long to validate themselves through the clothes they wear, the cars they drive, the latest disco dance they can perform. They also know that Nikki, like some cosmic mother, is trying to give them something all their own that no one can take away.

Nikki is trying, from one end of this country to the other, to say, "We can't use the nineteenth century as the arbiter of the twenty-first." She is quick to point out that her son will be thirty-five, her age, in the year 2004. And she's equally willing to admit she wants to be there to see it. Maybe that's not revolutionary, perhaps not even "Black," but it's Nikki. "I'm not young anymore," she says, and she speaks not only of years but aging. I hesitate to say mellowing, though I don't think Nikki would object to the term, because it implies, somehow, that the fire is gone. A good Bordeaux, of course, is no less a wine for the aging. But secretly Nikki is enjoying growing old. "I'm going to be fabulous at forty," she confides. "I just know it."

Her works and her words reflect her ever-widening curiosity about life. If Nikki had ever met Alexander the Great she would not have understood him as he sat sadly contemplating his life without further worlds to conquer. "There is always something to do," she tells the youngsters. "There are hungry people to feed, naked people to clothe, sick people to comfort and make well. And while I don't expect you to save the world I do think it's not asking too much for you to love those with whom you sleep, share the happiness of those whom you call friend, encourage those among you who are visionary and remove from your life those who offer you depression, despair and disrespect." It's a tall order that Nikki herself is constantly testing. But the joy is not the perfection but the endeavor. Life to Nikki will never be what we accomplish but what we tried. She, like a lot of us, gets frustrated with the fear and apathy of the seventies. Lowered expectations, thinking small, the litany about what we cannot expect do not enchant her. Life, she would agree with President James Earl Carter, Jr. ("I call him that because that's who he *is*") is not fair. "But if we aren't here to make it fairer then how does mankind justify his existence? We are not the smartest of the mammals; there is ample evidence that the dolphin, at least, is more intelligent. We are not the only animal with emotion; my dog Bruno loves me and wants me to love him. We are, however, the only creature on Earth who can convey feelings, who has the possibility of a collective memory. If mankind can remember for centuries backward we can plan for centuries forward. If mankind can *say* 'I feel,' we have an obligation *to* feel."

It can be baffling to those who have not experienced Nikki to understand her demanding simplicity. If you can do it you should. Long a believer in the future she can happily envision computers, little R2D2's, doing everything but writing poetry and making love. She "knows" they *feel* love; why can't they write poetry? "But that's what I do, Paula." It's a world she wants to share, no matter how imperfect or contradictory.

Nikki is one of the few living Black writers who has arranged to have her works catalogued. I recently saw the preliminary list from Boston University. "I would like my son, or anyone else who is interested, to know what we did, what we have gone through, to have someplace where they could go to find it." She is both intrigued and disappointed that the books being published on the sixties pay such scant notice to the Black contribution. "Blacks *made* the sixties—from Martin Luther King, Jr., and Malcolm X to LeRoi Jones and Rap Brown; and mostly all the wonderfully brave Black men, women and children who marched and prayed, who sat in and sat down, who said 'No' to slavery and 'Yes' to life. Yet all we see is the Tom Hayden–Chicago Seven mentality. The sixties are ours! And somebody's got to leave something." Nikki's necessity "to leave something" is not so much an act of egotism as a desire to get the record if not straight then on the right track. "There is, Paula," she said after reading a first draft of this, "an element of egotism too." But Nikki likes egos—hers and everyone else's. She once wrote a poem about it.

When I asked Ida Lewis if she had any suggestions for the writing of this introduction she said, "Write about Nikki's humanity—in the way she perceives things; in the way she talks about love in her poetry." I have never known anyone who cares so much and so intensely about the things she sees around her as Nikki. That speaks to her humanity and to her writing. Through the passion and the cynicism of the last two decades she has cared too much to have either a heartless mind or, just as importantly, a mindless heart. If Nikki, in her idealism, was a child of the sixties then now, in her realism, she is a woman of the seventies.

PAULA GIDDINGS
Paris, 1978

COTTON CANDY ON A RAINY DAY

Don't look now
I'm fading away
Into the gray of my mornings
Or the blues of every night

Is it that my nails
    keep breaking
Or maybe the corn
    on my second little piggy
Things keep popping out
    on my face
        or
    of my life

It seems no matter how
I try I become more difficult
    to hold
I am not an easy woman
    to want

They have asked
    the psychiatrists   psychologists   politicians and
    social workers
What this decade will be
    known for
There is no doubt   it is
    loneliness

If loneliness were a grape
   the wine would be vintage
If it were a wood
   the furniture would be mahogany
But since it is life   it is
   Cotton Candy
      on a rainy day
The sweet soft essence
   of possibility
Never quite maturing

I have prided myself
On being in the great tradition
   albeit circus
That the show must go on
Though in my community the vernacular is
   One Monkey Don't Stop the Show

We all line up
   at some midway point
To thread our way through
   the boredom and futility
Looking for the blue ribbon and gold medal

Mostly these are seen as food labels

We are consumed by people who sing
   the same old song   STAY:

                           as sweet as you are
                           in my corner

Or perhaps   *just a little bit longer*
But whatever you do   *don't change baby baby don't change*
Something needs to change
Everything   some say   will change
I need a change
    of pace   face   attitude and life
Though I long for my loneliness
I know I need something
Or someone
Or . . . . . .

I strangle my words as easily as I do my tears
I stifle my screams as frequently as I flash my smile
    it means nothing
I am cotton candy on a rainy day
    the unrealized dream of an idea unborn

I share with the painters the desire
To put a three-dimensional picture
On a one-dimensional surface

INTROSPECTION

she didn't like to think in abstracts
sadness happiness taking giving   all abstracts
she much preferred waxing the furniture
cleaning the shelves putting the plates away
something concrete to put her hands on
a job well done in a specific time span

her eyes were two bright shiny six guns
already cocked
prepared to go off at a moment's indiscretion
had she been a vietnam soldier or a mercenary
for Ian Smith   all the children and dogs and goodly
portions of grand old trees would have been demolished

she had lived both long and completely enough
not to be chained to truth
she was not pretty
she had no objections to the lies
lies were better than the silence that abounded
nice comfortable lies like   I need you
or   Gosh you look pretty this morning
the lies that make the lie of life real
or lies that make real life livable

she lived on the edge of an emotional abyss
or perhaps she lived in the well of a void
there were always things she wanted
like arms to hold her
eyes that understood
a friend to relax with
someone to touch
always   someone to touch

her life was a puzzle broken
into a hundred thousand little pieces
she didn't mind being emotionally disheveled
she was forever fascinated by putting the pieces
together   though most times
the center was empty

she never slept well
there wasn't a time
actually
when sleep refreshed her
perhaps it could have
but there were always dreams
or nightmares
and mostly her own acknowledgment
that she was meant to be tired

she lived
because she didn't know any better
she stayed alive
among the tired and lonely
not waiting   always wanting
needing a good night's rest

FORCED RETIREMENT

all problems being
as personal as they are
have to be largely
of our own making

i know i'm unhappy
most of the time
nothing an overdose
of sex won't cure of course
but since i'm responsible
i barely have an average
intake

on the other hand
i'm acutely aware
there are those suffering
from the opposite affliction

some people die of obesity
while others starve to death
some commit suicide
because they are bored
others because of pressure
the new norm is as elusive
as the old

granting problems coming
from within
are no less painful
than those out of our hands
i never really do worry
about atomic destruction
of the universe

though i can be quite vexed
that Namath and Ali don't retire
my father has to
and though he's never made a million
or even hundreds of thousands
he too enjoys his work
and is good at it
but more   goes
even when he doesn't
feel like it

people fear boredom
not because they are   bored
rather more from fear
of boring
though minds are either sharp
or dull
and bodies available
or not
and there's something else
that's never wrong
though never quite right
either

i've always thought the beautiful
are as pitiful
as the ugly
but the average is no guarantee
of happiness

i've always wandered a bit
not knowing if this is a function
of creeping menopause
or incipient loneliness
i no longer correct my habits

nothing makes sense
if we are just a collection of genes
on a freudian altar to the species
i don't like those theories
telling me why i feel as i do
behaviorisms never made sense
outside feeling

i could say i am black female
and bright
in a white male mediocre world
but that hardly explains why
i sit on the beaches of st croix
feeling so abandoned

THE NEW YORKERS

In front of the bank building
after six o'clock the gathering
of the bag people begins

In cold weather they huddle
around newspapers
when it is freezing they get
cardboard boxes

Someone said they are all rich eccentrics
Someone is   of course   crazy

The man and his buddy moved
to the truck port
in the adjoining building
most early evenings he visits
his neighbors awaiting
the return of his friend
from points unknown to me
they seem to be a spontaneous
combustion these night people
they evaporate during the light of day
only to emerge at evening glow
as if they had never been away

I am told there are people
who live underground
in the layer between the subways
and the pipes that run them
they have harnessed the steam
to heat their corner
and cook their food
though there is no electricity
making them effectively   moles

The twentieth century has seen
   two big wars and two small ones
   the automobile and the SST
   telephones and satellites in the sky
   man on the moon and spacecraft on Jupiter
How odd to also see the people
of New York City living
in the doorways of public buildings
as if this is an emerging nation
though of course it is

Look at the old woman
who sits on 57th Street and 8th Avenue
selling pencils
I don't know where she spends the night
she sits summer and winter
snow or rain humming
some white religious song
she must weigh over 250 pounds
the flesh on her legs has stretched
like a petite pair of stockings
onto a medium frame
beyond its ability to fit
there are tears and holes
of various purples in her legs
things and stuff ooze from them
drying and running again
there is never   though   a smell
she does not ask you to buy
a pencil nor will her eyes
condemn your health
it's easy really to walk by her
unlike the man in front
of Tiffany's she holds her pencils
near her knee

you take or not
depending upon your writing needs

He on the other hand is blind and walking
his german shepherd dog
his sign says THERE
BUT FOR THE GRACE OF GOD
GOES YOU and there is a long
explanation of his condition
It's rather easy for the Tiffany shopper
to see his condition
   he is Black

Uptown on 125th Street is an old blind Black woman
she is out only in good
      weather and clothes
her house is probably spotless
as southern ladies are wont to keep house
and her wig is always on straight
   You got something for me, she called
   What do you want, I asked
   What's yo name? I know yo family
   No, you don't, I said laughing   You don't know
     anything about me
   You that Eyetalian poet ain't you? I know yo voice. I seen you
     on television
I peered closely into her eyes
   You didn't see me or you'd know I'm black
   Let me feel yo hair   if you Black   Hold down yo head
I did and she did
   Got something for me, she laughed
   You felt my hair   that's good luck
   Good luck is money, chile   she said
   Good luck is money

CRUTCHES

it's not the crutches we decry
it's the need to move forward
though we haven't the strength

women aren't allowed to need
so they develop rituals
since we all know working hands idle
the devil
women aren't supposed to be strong
so they develop social smiles
and secret drinking problems
and female lovers whom they never touch
except in dreams

men are supposed to be strong
so they have heart attacks
and develop other women
who don't know their weaknesses
and hide their fears
behind male lovers
whom they religiously touch
each saturday morning on the basketball court
it's considered a sign of health doncha know
that they take such good care
of their bodies

i'm trying to say something about the human condition
maybe i should try again

if you broke an arm or leg
a crutch would be a sign of courage

people would sign your cast
and you could bravely explain
no it doesn't hurt—it just itches
but if you develop an itch
there are no salves to cover the area
in need of attention
and for whatever guilt may mean
we would feel guilty for trying
to assuage the discomfort
and even worse for needing the aid

i really want to say something about all of us
am i shouting   i want you to hear me

emotional falls always are
the worst
and there are no crutches
to swing back on

BOXES

i am in a box
on a tight string
subject to pop
without notice

everybody says how strong
i am

only black women
and white men
are truly free
they say

it's not difficult to see
how stupid they are

i would not reject
my strength
though its source
is not choice
but responsibility

i would not reject my light
though my wrinkles are also illuminated

something within demands
action
or words
if action is not possible

i am tired
of being boxed
muhammad ali must surely be pleased
that leon spinks relieved him

most of the time
i can't breathe
i smoke too much
to cover my fears
sometimes i pick
my nose to avoid
the breath i need

i do also do the same
injustice to my poems

i write because
i have to

POEM

i have considered
my reluctance
to be a fear of death
there are all sorts of reasons
i don't want to die
   responsibility to family
   obligations to friends
   dreams of future greatness
i close my eyes and chant
on airplanes to calm
my fleeting heart
since we are riding on air
my will is as necessary
as the pilot's abilities
to keep us afloat

i have felt that way
about other endeavors

however do we justify
our lives
the president of the united states
says Faith not deeds will determine
our salvation
that's probably why larry flynt
a stand-in for carter
is without his insides now
i have faith   of course
in the deeds i do
and see done
one really can't hate
the act but love
the actor
only jewish theater and american politics
would even contemplate
such a contradiction

however will we survive
the seventies

i seize on little things
you can tell a lot about people
by the way they comb their hair
or the way they don't look
you in the eye

am i discussing nixon
again

he went to humphrey's funeral
and opened his house
(2.50 per head)
for the public to see
i can't decide if anita bryant
should marry carter or nixon
they both are so bad
they deserve her

there must be something fun
worth sharing

there is a split
between the jewish and black community
the former didn't mind
until the latter put a name to it

i live in a city
that has turned into a garbage can
there is no disagreement
about that
there is some question

concerning the dog dung in the streets
as opposed to the dog dung in the administration

ahhhh   but you will say
how awful of the poet
such insinuations she does make
nobody is perfect
i do   after all   have
this   well   reluctance

A POEM OFF CENTER

how do poets write
so many poems
my poems get decimated
in the dishes the laundry
my sister is having another crisis
the bed has to be made
there is a blizzard on the way go to the grocery store
did you go to the cleaners
then a fuse blows
a fuse always has to blow
the women soon find themselves
talking either to babies or about them
no matter how careful we are
we end up giving tips
on the latest new improved cleaner
and the lotion that will take the smell away

if you write a political poem
you're anti-semitic
if you write a domestic poem
you're foolish
if you write a happy poem
you're unserious
if you write a love poem
you're maudlin
of course the only real poem
to write
is the go to hell writing establishment poem
but the readers never know who
you're talking about which brings us back
to point one

i feel   i think   sorry for the women
they have no place to go
it's the same old story blacks
hear all the time
if it's serious a white man
would do it
when it's serious
he will
everything from writing a poem
to sweeping the streets
to cooking the food
as long as his family doesn't eat it

it's a little off center
this life we're leading
maybe i shouldn't feel sorry
for myself
but the more i understand women
the more i do

THE WINTER STORM

somewhere there was a piano playing
but not in the bar
where she was sitting

somewhere across the candlelights
like a ship threading its way
through the morning fog
two people were surely moving
toward completion

she knew she had feelings
that were unfulfilled

there must certainly be a revolution
somewhere
but she couldn't see it
the idea of fulfillment baffled her

most assuredly she remembered

the sheets were clean
and he was tender
it was an accident
that rush of red wine starting with her toes
that came over her ending with a sigh
she had always hated people
who had to talk and instruct
or give indiscreet encouragement
she had laughed and laughed
what a marvelous thing you have discovered
she told him

she looked to see if anyone was happy
in the bar in which she was sitting

how many aeons had it been
how many men
enough to make her secure
in her desirability
too many to allow herself to say
she loved them all
remembering the names was the hardest
though she always retained the ability
to rate them
what indeed made sex
so fascinating to everyone
at best it's a tooth in a pain
that rubbing the gums will ease
at worst it's a desire denied
like the eyes closing
to the evening's sunset

she looked and crossed her support-hosed legs
in the bar with the music just out of reach

one always remembers passion
whether fantasy or fact
that rush of pure glandular energy
what really did she feel

she straightened her gray flannel panel skirt
pulling her gray silk blouse tight against her breasts
rubbing her left arm with the square gold band
against the chill that settled on the right
she looked around at the lonely faces
in the bar without the music

what made people interested
in other people
in whom they have no interest
but yes she recalled
as the drink was served
there is an energy crisis that's why
i'm having this drink
amid a raging storm outside
there is one inside too
and spring will not lessen
its ferocity

unconsciously as black women
are wont to do
she hummed a tune and patted her foot
to the gospel beat
the tips of the black pumps were a grayish white
the ice and salt having taken
their measure

she examined her nails
noting the cuticles needed trimming
a dim reflection from the mirror on the wall
showed her the face and form of a coward
life   she justified   is not heroic
but survival

tonight through the storm
she would sit in a bar
with only the music in her head

in the morning   for sure   she would go
home

AGE

we tend to fear old age
as some sort of disorder   that can be cured
with the proper brand of aspirin
or perhaps a bit of Ben Gay for the shoulders
it does   of course   pay to advertise

one hates the idea of the first gray hair
a shortness of breath
devastating blows to the ego
indications we are doing
what comes naturally

it's almost laughable
that we detest aging
when we first become aware
we want it
little girls of four or five push
with eyes shining brightly at gram or mommy
the lie that they are seven or eight
little girls at ten worry
that a friend has gotten her monthly
and she has not
little girls of twelve
can be socially crushed
by lack of nobs on their chests

little boys of fourteen want
to think they want
a woman
the little penis that simply won't erect
is shattering to their idea of manhood
if perhaps they get a little peach fuzz
on their faces they may survive
adolescence proving there may indeed be life
after high school

the children begin to play   older
without knowing the price is   weariness

age teaches us that our virtues
are neither virtuous nor our vices
foul
age doesn't matter   really
what frightens is mortality
it dawns upon us that we can die
at some point it occurs we surely shall

it is not death we fear
but the loss of youth
not the youth of our teens
where most of the thinking took place
somewhere between the navel and the knee
but the youth of our thirties where career
decisions were going well
and we were respected for our abilities
or the youth of our forties
where our decisions proved if not right
then not wrong either
and the house   after all   is half paid

it may simply be that work
is so indelibly tied
to age that the loss
of work brings the depression
of impending death
there are so many   too many
who have never worked
and therefore for whom death
is a constant companion

as lack of marriage
lowers divorce rates
lack of life
prevents death
the unwillingness to try
is worse than any failure

in youth our ignorance gives us courage
with age our courage gives us hope
with hope we learn that man is more
than the sum of what he does
we also are what we wish we did
and age teaches us
that even that doesn't matter

BECAUSE

i wrote a poem
for you because
you are
my little boy

i wrote a poem
for you because
you are
my darling daughter

and in this poem
i sang a song
that says
as time goes on
i am you
and you are me
and that's how life
goes on

THEIR FATHERS

i will be bitter
when i grow old
i have seen the weakness
of our race
though i   as with many others
am reluctant
to give it name

each day i face ⌐
the world through fantasies
of past glories
who i deceive i am not ⌐
at all sure
   not myself
   not the whites above
   surely even the children ⌐
know the sterility
of their fathers

there are both reasons
and excuses .
none are lacking in
understanding the causes
a cold front meeting
a warm mass of air ⌐
causes rain also
but that reason offers
less comfort
than a simple raincoat

mankind alone
among the mammals
communicates with his species
justification for his behavior.
none among us lack compassion

or understanding or even sympathy
emotion is not a response
to inaction ⌐
and undoubtedly there are those
who are so unfeeling
they cannot represent mental
or emotional health .
we have seen the Germans
and the Israeli reaction
and the Palestinian response⌐
in our own time .
we know the truth
of the Africans and Indians
we know we have only begun
the horror that is waiting
south of our borders
and south of our latitude
blood perhaps should not
all ways be the answer
but perhaps it always is

my people have suffered
so much for so long
we are pitiful
in our misery

we boost our spirits
by changing our minds ⌐
rather than our condition .
blacks are still rather cheap
to purchase ⌐
    unemployment insurance
    a grant for a program programmed to fail
    enough seed money to insure bankruptcy .
my people like magnificent race ⌐
horses have blinders
there is always talk
of the mighty past
but no plans ⌐

for a decent future,
if no man is an island
black americans stand to prove
a people can be a peninsula
we are extended   phallic like   in an ocean
of whiteness
though that is not our problem
our extension like arms on
the body or legs on
a trunk is essential to balance
one neither walks nor stands without
extensions
one is not black without white
nor male without female
what is true of the mass is no less
true of the individual

someone said the only emotion
black men show
is rage or anger
which is only partly true
the only rage and anger
they show are to those
who would want to love them
and bear their children
and with them walk into the future,
why do we
who have offered expectation
have to absorb pain

i will grow bitter
in old age
because life is not a problem,
but a process
and there are no formulas
to our situation .

the dinosaurs became extinct
ripened fruit falls from the bough
and i grow tired of hoping

it's only natural
that bitterness rests within
my spirit
the air is polluted
streams are poisoned
and i have seen the hollow look
of hatred in the dull
worn faces
of their fathers

LIFE CYCLES

she realized
she wasn't one
of life's winners
when   she wasn't sure
life to her was some dark
dirty secret that
like some unwanted child
too late for an abortion
was to be borne
alone

she had so many private habits
she would masturbate sometimes
she always picked her nose when upset
she liked to sit with silence
in the dark
sadness is not an unusual state
for the black woman
or writers

she took to sneaking drinks
a habit which displeased her
both for its effects
and taste
yet eventually sleep
would wrestle her in triumph
onto the bed

she was nervous
when he was there
and anxious
when he wasn't
life   to her
was a crude cruel joke
played on the livers

she boxed her life
like a special private seed
planting it in her emotional garden
to see what weeds
would rise
to strangle
her

ADULTHOOD II

There is always something
of the child
in us that wants
a strong hand to hold
through the hungry season
of growing up

when she was a child
summer lasted forever
and christmas seemed never
to come
now her bills from easter
usually are paid
by the 4th of july
in time to buy the ribs
and corn and extra bag of potatoes
for salad

the pit is cleaned
and labor day is near
time to tarpaulin
the above ground pool

thanksgiving turkey
is no sooner soup
than the children's shoes
wear thin saying
christmas is near   again
bringing the february letters asking
"did you forget
us last month"

her life looks occasionally
as if it's owed to some
machine
and the only winning point
she musters is to tear
mutilate and twist
the cards demanding information
payment
and a review of her credit worthiness

she sits sometimes
in her cubicled desk
and recalls her mother
did the same things
what we have been given
we are now expected to return
and she smiles

HABITS

i haven't written a poem in so long
i may have forgotten how
unless writing a poem
is like riding a bike
or swimming upstream
or loving you
it may be a habit that once acquired
is never lost

but you say i'm foolish
of course you love me
but being loved of course
is not the same as being loved because
or being loved despite
or being loved

if you love me why
do i feel so lonely
and why do i always wake up alone
and why am i practicing
not having you to love
i never loved you that way

if being loved by you is accepting always
        getting the worst
        taking the least
        hearing the excuse
and never being called when you say you will
then it's a habit
like smoking cigarettes
or brushing my teeth when i awake
something i do without
thinking
but something without
which i could just as well do

most habits occur
because of laziness
we overdrink
because our friends do
we overeat
because our parents think
we need more flesh
on the bones
and perhaps my worst habit
is overloving
and like most who live
to excess
i will be broken
in two
by my unwillingness
to control my feelings

but i sit writing
a poem
about my habits
which while it's not
a great poem
is mine
and some habits
like smiling at children
or giving a seat to an old person
should stay
if for no other reason
than their civilizing
influence

which is the ultimate
habit
i need
to acquire

FASCINATIONS

finding myself still fascinated
by the falls and rapids
i nonetheless prefer the streams
contained within the bountiful brown shoreline
i prefer the inland waters
to the salty seas
knowing that journeys end
as they begin
the sailor and his sail
the lover and her beloved
the light of day and night's darkness

i walk the new york streets
the heat rising in waves
to singe my knees
my head is always down
for i no longer look for you
usually i am cold no matter
what the temperature
i hunch my hands in the pockets of my pants
hoping you will be home
when i get there

i know i'm on dangerous ground
i misread your smile all year
assured that you and therefore everything
was all right
i wade from the quiet
of your presence into the turbulence
of your emotions
i have now understood a calm day
does not preclude a stormy evening
con edison after all went out
why shouldn't you
and though it took longer than anyone thought

60

the lights did come back on
why shouldn't yours
electricity is a product of the sea
as much as the air
coming from turbulence
as much as generators

if you were a pure bolt
of fire cutting the skies
i'd touch you risking my life
not because i'm brave or strong
but because i'm fascinated
by what the outcome will be

GUS
(for my father)

He always had pretty legs
Even now   though he has gotten fat
His legs have kept their shape

He swam
Some men get those legs from tennis
But he swam
In a sink-or-swim mud hole somewhere
In Alabama

When he was a young man
More than half a century ago
Talent was described by how well
A thing was done   not by whom
That is   considering
That Black men weren't considered
One achieved on merit

The fact that he is short
Was an idea late reaching his consciousness
He hustled the ball on the high school court
Well enough to win a college scholarship
Luckily for me
Since that's where he met my mother

I have often tried to think lately
When I first met him
I don't remember
He was a stranger
As Black or perhaps responsible fathers
Are wont to be

He worked three jobs   a feat
Without precedence though not unknown
In the hills of West Virginia or the Red Clay of Georgia
What happens to a dream
When it must tunnel under
Langston says it might explode
It might also just die
Shriveling to the here and now
Confusing the dreamer til he no longer knows
Whether he is awake or asleep

Before we ourselves:
    Meet the man
    Lie to the bill collectors
    Don't know where the mortgage payment is coming from
It's difficult to understand
A weakness

Before our mettle is tested
We easily consider ourselves strong
Before we see our children want
Not elaborate things
But a christmas bike or easter shoes
It's easy to say
what should have been done

Before we see our own possibility shrink
Back into the unclonable cell
From which dreams spring
It's easy to condemn

If the first sign of spring is the swallows
Then the first sign of maturity is the pride
We gulp when we realize
There are few choices in life
That are clear
Seldom is good pitted against evil
Or even better against best
Mostly it's bad versus worse
And while some may intone
     life is not fair
"Choice" by definition implies
Equally attractive alternatives
Or mutually exclusive experiences

Boxers protect themselves from blows
    with heavily greased shoulders
Football players wear helmets
Joggers have specially made shoes
    to absorb the shocks
The problem with the Life game
For unprotected players
Is not what you don't have
But what you can't give
Though ultimately there is the understanding
That even nothing is something
As long as you are there
To give the nothing   personally

Black men grow inverse
To the common experience

He grew younger as his children left home
He has both time and money to buy
The toys he never had
Lawn mowers   saws   garden equipment   CB's
    Stereos
Whatever is new and exciting
He smiles more often too
And his legs are still
quite exceptional
For a Grandfather

CHOICES

if i can't do
what i want to do
then my job is to not
do what i don't want
to do

it's not the same thing
but it's the best i can
do

if i can't have
what i want   then
my job is to want
what i've got
and be satisfied
that at least there
is something more
to want

since i can't go
where i need
to go   then i must   go
where the signs point
though always understanding
parallel movement
isn't lateral

when i can't express
what i really feel
i practice feeling
what i can express
and none of it is equal
i know
but that's why mankind
alone among the mammals
learns to cry

PHOTOGRAPHY

the eye we are told
is a camera
but the film is the heart
not the brain
and our hands joining
those that reach
develop the product

it's easy sitting in the sun
to forget that cold exists
let alone envelops
the lives of people
it's easy sitting in the sun
to forget the ice and ravages
of winter yet
there are those who would have
no other season
it's always easy when thinking
we have the best to assume
others covet it
yet surf or sea each has
its lovers and its meaning
for love

watching the red sun bleed
into the ocean
one thinks of the beauty that fire brings
if the eye is a camera and the film is the heart
then the photo assistant is god

THE BEEP BEEP POEM

I should write a poem
but there's almost nothing
that hasn't been said
and said and said
beautifully, ugly, blandly
excitingly
    stay in school
    make love not war
    death to all tyrants
    where have all the flowers gone
and don't they understand at kent state
the troopers will shoot . . . again

i could write a poem
because i love walking
in the rain
and the solace of my naked
body in a tub of warm water
cleanliness may not be next
to godliness but it sure feels
good

i wrote a poem
for my father but it was so constant
i burned it up
he hates change
and i'm baffled by sameness

i composed a ditty
about encore american and worldwide news
but the editorial board
said no one would understand it
as if people have to be tricked
into sensitivity
though of course they do

i love to drive my car
hours on end
along back country roads
i love to stop for cider and apples and acorn squash
three for a dollar
i love my CB when the truckers talk
and the hum of the diesel in my ear
i love the aloneness of the road
when I ascend descending curves
the power within my toe delights me
and i fling my spirit down the highway
i love the way i feel
when i pass the moon and i holler to the stars
i'm coming through

Beep Beep

A POEM FOR ED AND ARCHIE

I dreamed of you last night
standing near the Drugstore on the St.-Germain-des-Prés
You popped out of the pastry shop
wiping some exotic créme from your lips
showing off your new cigarette holder
"Got one yet?"
and your smile lit up the city of lights
Southern men cannot be generalized about
I know you all as liars and lynchers
I have accepted the myth that though you may wear a suit
beneath it the blood runs hot
and your hair   so similar to those whom Darwin said were
     all our ancestors   mats against your heaving chest
It's unpatriotic not to smoke tobacco
we both agreed   at least in North Carolina
and poor Ed   who will some day be a great man
just sat there confused

without laughter what is the purpose
my ancestors once worked for yours
involuntarily
and I laugh because it is only what happened
not nearly the truth

I've seen Paris and you've seen me
and last night in my dream
we both smiled

WOMAN

she wanted to be a blade
of grass amid the fields
but he wouldn't agree
to be the dandelion

she wanted to be a robin singing
through the leaves
but he refused to be
her tree

she spun herself into a web
and   looking for a place to rest
turned to him
but he stood straight
declining to be her corner

she tried to be a book
but he wouldn't read

she turned herself into a bulb
but he wouldn't let her grow

she decided to become
a woman
and though he still refused
to be a man
she decided it was all
right

SPACE

a flying saucer landed
in my living room
i too am an astronaut
having applied for my own space
i welcomed the visitor
i need something intelligent
to talk to   not for long
but maybe just through dinner

not being afraid
of what i don't know
i unanxiously awaited the emergence

should i call him a space man
or might not it be a woman
probably not
her menses on jupiter
no less than earth
causes excuses for exclusion

should i shake hands
and offer a glass of white wine
i always wanted to know space
people but how do we proceed

i think i should tell you
she reported as she stepped from her craft
you possibly are not seeing me
depending upon the solar year
you may only be seeing my aura

don't worry i assured her
happy it was a woman
depending upon my aura
you are most likely only seeing
my solar years

we sat down
to talk

POEM (for EMA)

though i do wonder
why you intrigue me
i recognize that an exceptional moth
is always drawn
to an exceptional flame

you're not at all what you appear
to be
though not so very different

i've not learned
the acceptable way of saying
you fascinate me
I've not even learned
how to say i like you
without frightening people
away

sometimes I see things
that aren't really there
like warmth and kindness
when people are mean
but sometimes i see things
like fear and want to soothe it
or fatigue and want to share it
or love and want to receive it

is that weird
you think everyone is weird
though you're not really hypocritical
you just practice not being
what you want to be
and fail to understand
how others would dare
to be otherwise
that's weird to me

flames don't flicker
forever
and moths are born to be burned

it's an unusual way
to start a friendship
but nothing lasts forever

THE ROSE BUSH
(for Gordon)

i know i haven't grown but
i don't fit beneath the rose
bush by my grandmother's porch

i couldn't have grown so much though
i don't see why the back of the couch
doesn't hide me from my sister

the lightning that would flash
on summer days brought shouts
of you children be still   the lightning's
gonna get you

we laughed my cousins and sister and i
at the foolish old people
and their backward superstitions
though lightning struck me
in new york city
and i ran
to or from what   i'm not sure
but i was hit
and now i don't fit
beneath the rose bushes
anymore
anyway   they're gone

PATIENCE

there are sounds
which shatter
the staleness of lives
transporting the shadows
into the dreams

raindrops falling
on leaves shatter
the dust of the city
as soap washed off
bodies shatters
the complacent dirt

she waited for him
to take away that quiet

she waited for his call
with the patience of a slave
woman quilting or a jewish mother
simmering chicken broth

there would be no other
sound than his voice
to shatter the quiet
of her heart

she waited for him
to come

MAKE UP

we make up our faces
for lots of reasons
to go to the movies
or some junior prom
to see ice hockey
or watch the Dodgers come home again
defeated

going to the grocery store
only requires lipstick
while a bridge game
can mean a quick trip
to the hairdresser for a touch up

i clean my make up
before going to bed
alone
and if my mood is foul
i spray the sheets
with Ultra Ban

most faces are made up
before the public is faced
whether male female or child
it's always so appropriate
don'tcha know
to put a little mascara
around the eyes

we make up fantasies
to face life
we need to believe

we are good on the job
or at least in the bed

we make up lies
to impress people
who are making up lies
to impress us
and if either took all
the make up off
life would not be
worth living

we make up excuses
to say i'm sorry *that*
forgive me *because*
and after all didn't i tell you
why

and i make up with you
because you aren't strong
enough to reach out
to say
come home   i need you

WINTER

Frogs burrow the mud
snails bury themselves
and I air my quilts
preparing for the cold

Dogs grow more hair
mothers make oatmeal
and little boys and girls
take Father John's Medicine

Bears store fat
chipmunks gather nuts
and I collect books
For the coming winter

YOU ARE THERE

i shall save my poems
for the winter of my dreams
i look forward to huddling
in my rocker with my life
i wonder what i'll contemplate
lovers—certainly those
i can remember
and knowing my life
you'll be there

you'll be there in the cold
like a Siamese on my knee
proud purring when you let me stroke you

you'll be there in the rain
like an umbrella over my head
sheltering me from the damp mist

you'll be there in the dark
like a lighthouse in the fog
seeing me through troubled waters

you'll be there in the sun
like coconut oil on my back
to keep me from burning

i shall save a special poem
for you to say
you always made me smile
and even though i cried sometimes
you said i will not let you
down

my rocker and i on winter's porch
will never be sad if you're gone
the winter's cold has been stored
against
you will always be
there

A STATEMENT ON CONSERVATION

Scarcity in oil and gas
Can bring about a cold spell
No one cares if you conserve
As long as you can pay well

Cash is not the only tool
To purchase what we need
Dollar bills and jingling change
Are very cheap indeed

Buying power in our world
Speaks to white illusion
Understanding what I need
I've come to this conclusion

   Love is in short supply
   Like leaves on a winter vine
   Whether it's right or whether it's wrong
   I'll pay the price for mine

Spring is late and summer soon
Will come in with its heat wave
We will all need energy
Unless we have a cool cave

I don't mind the cold or heat
And I've got a reason
Love when it's spread all around
Can tackle any season

TURNING (I need a better title)

she often wondered why people spoke
of gaining years as turning
when she celebrated her thirtieth birthday she knew
she had turned though
she hadn't gained

the rain turned on her windowsill
and it didn't gain
and he like her face gaining
wrinkles
turned indifferent

she became happier without
the big apartment
the stereo components
and the ten pounds she shed
while adjusting to the loss
of his love

her fault lay
in her honesty
it was always his sexiness
that held her not
his arms
it was his lovemaking not
his love she missed

she compacted her
life into one
tiny room with kitchen   bed and roaches
in the four corners which contained nothing
that couldn't be stolen
or left in case
she had to run
for her sanity

so she turned thirty-one
with all
the introspections that nothing
not even them was meant
not to turn
and from that understanding
she gained
knowledge

A RESPONSE
(to the rock group Foreigner)

you say i'm as cold
as ice
but ice is good
for a burn
if you were a woman
you would have known that
and rubbed me
the right way
to let me cool
your passion

A POEM OF FRIENDSHIP

We are not lovers
because of the love
we make
but the love
we have

We are not friends
because of the laughs
we spend
but the tears
we save

I don't want to be near you
for the thoughts we share
but the words we never have
to speak

I will never miss you
because of what we do
but what we are
together

BEING AND NOTHINGNESS
(to quote a philosopher)

i haven't done anything
meaningful in so long
it's almost meaningful
to do nothing

i suppose i could fall in love
or at least in line
since i'm so discontented
but that takes effort
and i don't want to exert anything
neither my energy nor my emotions

i've always prided myself
on being a child of the sixties
and we are all finished
so that makes being
nothing

THE MOON SHINES DOWN

the moon shines down
on new york city
while i smile over
at you

the moon is still
against the night
and i am still
against you

surely you must sometimes wonder
won't i ever go home
surely you must sometimes say
poet please leave me alone

but my bad rhyme
and love of night
retain me here with you
and though it's so sad to admit
without you what would i do

of course you are no panacea
for my lack of friends
but if i were a hallmark card
here's where we'd begin

the moon shines down
on new york city
while i smile over
at you

THAT DAY

if you've got the key
then i've got the door
let's do what we did
when we did it before

if you've got the time
i've got the way
let's do what we did
when we did it all day

you get the glass
i've got the wine
we'll do what we did
when we did it overtime

if you've got the dough
then i've got the heat
we can use my oven
til it's warm and sweet

i know i'm bold
coming on like this
but the good things in life
are too good to be missed

now time is money
and money is sweet
if you're busy baby
we can do it on our feet

we can do it on the floor
we can do it on the stair
we can do it on the couch
we can do it in the air

we can do it in the grass
and in case we get an itch
i can scratch it with my left hand
cause i'm really quite a witch

if we do it once a month
we can do it in time
if we do it once a week
we can do it in rhyme
if we do it every day
we can do it everyway
we can do it like we did it
when we did it
that day